Constitutional Origins
of the Federal Judiciary

Federal Judicial Center
Federal Judicial History Office
2005

Contents

Introduction, 1

Part I. Constitutional Origins of the Federal Judiciary—Talking Points, 1
1. Establishing an Independent Judiciary for the New Nation, 1
2. Models for the Federal Judiciary, 1
3. Proposals at the Federal Convention, 2
4. Defining the Judiciary, 2
5. Public Debates on the Proposed Constitution, 5
6. Ratification, 7
7. Judiciary Act of 1789, 7
8. The Bill of Rights, 8

Part II. Constitutional Origins of the Federal Judiciary—Suggested Discussion Questions, 9

Part III. Constitutional Origins of the Federal Judiciary—Historical Documents, 10

In the Federal Convention, 1787, 10
1. The Virginia Plan on the Judiciary, 10
2. Appointment Power, 10
3. Council of Revision, 12
4. Article III of the U.S. Constitution, 14

The Anti-Federalist Critique, 15
5. Letters of "Brutus", 15
6. Letters from the Federal Farmer, 16

The Federalist Defense, 17
7. Federalist 78 (Excerpt), 17
8. Federalist 80 (Excerpt), 17
9. Federalist 81 (Excerpt), 18

Bibliography, 19

Introduction

This teaching module was developed by the Federal Judicial Center to support judges and court staff who want to speak to various groups about the history of an independent federal judiciary. It focuses on the Constitutional Convention of 1787 and the establishment of the judicial branch of government. Other modules in this series examine the creation of the federal judicial system and debates on judicial independence. Each module includes four components: background discussion to serve as talking points; a Powerpoint presentation that can be downloaded to provide a visual guide to the speakers' remarks; a list of suggested discussion questions; and selections from historical documents that can be used in discussion with the audience or incorporated in the speakers' remarks.

Part I. Constitutional Origins of the Federal Judiciary—Talking Points

1. Establishing an Independent Judiciary for the New Nation

    At the Constitutional Convention of 1787, the delegates shared a commitment to an independent judiciary. They agreed that an indispensable part of any well-organized republican government was a separate and coequal judicial branch that would serve alongside the executive and legislative branches. But the delegates did not arrive in Philadelphia with a fully developed plan for the federal judiciary. Most were more concerned with the provisions for a national legislature and the executive or with the balance of federal and state authority. The constitutional outline of the nation's court system emerged over the summer, often in response to decisions the delegates made about the structure of the executive and legislative branches. As the Convention delegates proceeded with their work, the importance of the federal judiciary became more and more evident, although much of the institutional organization we think of as central to the federal court system was not defined until the First Congress convened in 1789.

2. Models for the Federal Judiciary

    The delegates to the Federal Convention, like many Americans, accepted certain values associated with the British judicial system. Since the late-seventeenth century, independence of judges in Great Britain had been secured through provisions for service "during good behavior," which generally meant lifetime tenure.

Beginning in 1776, the newly independent states dismantled the colonial court systems that were generally under the control of royal governors and established in their place judiciaries that would be important models for the Federal Convention. Virginia's constitution was the first to establish the judiciary as one of three independent branches of government. Some states provided for judges to serve during good behavior and some mandated a fixed salary for judges. In the 1780s, several state courts asserted the authority to judge state laws in violation of the state constitution, and legal writers proposed ways to make the judiciaries more independent of the legislature as well as the executive. The framers would look to the experience of the state courts for lessons about the best ways to make a judiciary independent and to ensure a proper separation of powers.

The framers of the Constitution had no practical model of a court to serve the whole nation. The only court established under the Articles of Confederation, which served as the first national government, was the Court of Appeals in Cases of Captures. This body had very limited jurisdiction; it dealt only with the capture of enemy ships and had no enforcement powers. The proper role of an independent, national judiciary was a largely unexplored topic when the Federal Convention convened.

3. Proposals at the Federal Convention

The Federal Convention began its discussion of a new constitution with consideration of the so-called Virginia Plan submitted by Edmund Randolph and drafted by James Madison. Madison proposed that the legislature be authorized to establish one or more supreme courts (perhaps with different jurisdiction) that would hear appeals of cases of national interest, and inferior courts that would serve as trial courts for national issues. Judges of these courts would hold office during good behavior, be appointed by the Congress, and receive a fixed salary that could not be increased or decreased during their service. A council of revision, made up of the executive and some federal judges, would review state and federal laws and veto those they believed violated the Constitution or even those they considered harmful.

4. Defining the Judiciary

Early in the Convention, delegates agreed that there would be a single supreme court and one or more inferior courts, but that decision about inferior courts was soon reversed. During the remaining three months of the Convention, the delegates engaged in recurring debates on questions related to the federal judiciary: who would appoint judges? what would be the term of office for judges? what provisions would be made for judges' salaries? who would exercise judicial review of state and federal laws? and what would be the relationship between federal and state courts?

Appointment—Some delegates, like James Wilson of Pennsylvania, recommended appointment by the executive as a protection against the intrigues associated with a large legislature. Many more supported appointment by the legislature or by the Senate alone. John Rutledge of South Carolina, who later served as a Supreme Court justice, feared that concentrating the appointment power in the hands of a single executive would lead to monarchy. Roger Sherman of Connecticut thought appointment by the Senate would ensure that judges were drawn from every part of the country. Madison feared that many members of the full Congress would not have the experience to assess the qualifications for a judge, and he initially preferred appointment by the more exclusive membership of the Senate.

Nathaniel Gorham, a delegate from Massachusetts, suggested the mode of judicial appointment that his state had used since the colonial period: nomination by the executive and approval by the smaller branch of the legislature. Once the convention decided that the Senate would represent states equally, Madison suggested that the President be authorized to appoint judges but that the Senate be given the right to veto the appointment by a vote of two-thirds of the members. Only in the final two weeks of the convention did the delegates agree that federal judges, like ambassadors and other appointed officers, would be appointed by the President with the advice and consent of the Senate.

Tenure and removal—The delegates generally agreed that judges should have tenure with good behavior, but it was more difficult to decide what was the proper standard of good behavior and who would determine when judges did not meet that standard. Many of the early state constitutions followed the British model and provided for the removal of judges by the executive branch upon recommendation of the legislature. When John Dickinson of Delaware proposed a similar removal process for federal judges, several delegates worried that the judges would then be vulnerable to political pressures. Gouvernor Morris of New York thought removal of judges for violation of a standard of good behavior required some form of trial. With no further debate in the full convention, the authors of the final draft of the Constitution inserted a provision for removal of judges only through impeachment by the House of Representatives and conviction of "high crimes and misdemeanors" in a trial conducted by the Senate.

Salary—The delegates understood that the salary provisions for judges would be a key to protecting judicial independence, and the Virginia Plan proposed that judges would receive a fixed, regular salary that could not be increased or reduced. No one challenged the provision to protect judges from any reduction in salary, which was seen as an essential protection against political pressure from the legislature. But the absence of pay increases also could make the judges dependent, warned Gouvernor Morris, who believed that judicial salaries must be regulated by the costs of living, or, as he put it, "the manners & the style of the living in a Country." Benjamin Franklin wanted the option of increasing judges' salaries if the business of the courts increased. Charles Cotesworth Pinckney of South Carolina argued that large salaries would be necessary to attract "men of the first talents." Madison feared that if a pay raise for judges were pending before the Congress, judges might be reluctant to rule against the government or the interests of individual members of Congress. Madison suggested judicial pay might be pegged to the price of a familiar commodity like wheat, but a large majority of state delegations insisted on leaving open an option for judicial pay raises.

Judicial Review—The Convention's longest debate involving the judiciary focused on Madison's proposal for a council of revision. Following the model of the New York state constitution, Madison envisioned a council made up of the President and a group of judges who would review all legislation and have the authority to suggest revisions or to veto an act. The council would also have had authority to review Congress's recommendation for the disallowance of state legislation. Madison, who believed that the natural tendency of a republican legislature was "to absorb all power into its vortex," thought it was essential to bring the executive and judicial branches together as a check on improper or unjust legislation. He so strongly advocated this role of the judiciary that he brought the motion up twice after the Convention had rejected it.

Many delegates thought it would violate the separation of powers to join the executive and the judicial in this way. Judges should not have a role in the formation of policy, said Nathaniel Gorham. Caleb Strong of Massachusetts feared that the judges' role on a council of revision would undermine their credibility when they reviewed laws that were challenged in court. John Rutledge thought judges should never give an opinion on legislation until it was law. The Convention repeatedly rejected Madison's proposal and left the President with the sole authority to veto legislation. Although the Constitution made no reference to judicial review, the debate on the council of revision made clear that many delegates believed the council was unnecessary because they expected the federal judiciary to exercise the power of judicial review to declare laws invalid.

Organization and Jurisdiction—The proposed Constitution defined the potential jurisdiction of the Supreme Court and the federal judiciary, but left unanswered many of the questions that had divided the delegates. Madison's original plan proposed a series of inferior federal courts to serve as trial courts, but many delegates, like William Paterson, proposed that the state courts serve as the courts of first instance, or trial courts, in cases raising federal issues. After the delegates rejected a proposal to establish inferior federal courts, they accepted the proposal of Madison and James Wilson to give the Congress authority to establish inferior courts, thus leaving open the option that state courts might serve as trial courts for many questions arising under federal laws or the Constitution. It would be up to the new Congress to organize the court system.

The Constitution's grant of jurisdiction to federal courts extended to all cases "in law and equity" arising under the Constitution, federal laws, and treaties. Federal jurisdiction also included cases related to foreign diplomats, admiralty and maritime issues, disputes between states, and disputes between citizens of different states. With little recorded debate, the delegates in the closing days of the Convention accepted language that guaranteed a trial by jury in criminal trials, but the delegates rejected pleas to extend the guarantee of jury trials to civil cases. Also with little debate, the delegates accepted a provision for appeals to the Supreme Court "both as to Law and Fact." By defining the range of federal jurisdiction, the Convention implicitly recognized that state courts would retain full jurisdiction over many legal questions.

5. Public Debates on the Proposed Constitution

Once the proposed Constitution was presented to the states for ratification, critics of the charter, known as the Anti-Federalists, offered the public a critique of the proposed judiciary, which they feared would weaken the authority of states and undermine legal rights secured by the establishment of independent state governments. The supporters of the Constitution, known as Federalists, responded with explanations of how important an independent judiciary would be for the success of a national government.

For opponents of the Constitution, the judiciary symbolized the expansive power of a national government that they feared would soon overwhelm the states. Anti-Federalists frequently warned that the federal judiciary would "absorb" or "swallow" the state courts, even the states themselves. The Constitution's broad definition of federal jurisdiction would allow judges and lawyers to expand the reach of the courts as far as they wished. Federal jurisdiction over suits between citizens of different states was seen as particularly threatening to state courts. The power and independence of the judges, who could not be removed for errors of decision or judgment, was, in the words of a leading Anti-Federalist writer, "unprecedented in a free country."

The outline of the federal judiciary seemed to remove the courts from the local connections that many Americans believed were essential to the preservation of civil liberties. Even if a federal trial court were established in each state and the Supreme Court met in various locations, according to Anti-Federalists, the remoteness of federal courts would deprive most citizens of justice. The distance to a federal court would make legal proceedings too expensive and render justice "unattainable by a great part of the community," according to George Mason. Jury trials protected the rights of defendants only if the jury were drawn from the local community, and this would be impractical in a federal court.

Anti-Federalists saw in the proposed Constitution two grave threats to the right to a trial by jury, which they saw as the most important means of insuring popular participation in the judicial process and protecting individual liberties. Despite the guarantee of a jury trial in criminal cases, the absence of any reference to jury trials in civil cases raised the specter of a civil law system in which "a few judges . . . possess all the power in the judiciary." The provision for appeals to the Supreme Court on the basis of challenges to the facts as well as the law raised additional fears of the possible retrial of criminal cases without a jury. The Constitution's failure to explicitly protect traditional rights to a jury trial became one of the most compelling criticisms raised by the Anti-Federalists.

The *Federalist* essays of Alexander Hamilton offered the most notable defense of an independent judiciary and a persuasive answer to many of the Anti-Federalist criticisms of the proposed court system. In his famous phrase, the judiciary would be the branch of government "least dangerous to the political rights of the constitution." The judges had no means of coercion, like the executive control of the military or the Congress's power over spending, and the judiciary would in practice be dependent on the executive for the enforcement of its decisions. What appeared to the Anti-Federalists as a virtually unchecked judicial authority was, Hamilton argued, absolutely essential to protect the liberties of the people under a government with constitutionally limited powers. The Constitution, once ratified by the states, would be the ultimate expression of the popular will, and it was the judiciary's responsibility to enforce that popular will when it was violated by legislation that was contrary to the Constitution. Only with the twin protections of tenure during good behavior and salaries that could not be reduced would judges be able to enforce the Constitution free of pressure from the other branches of government or temporary popular majorities.

Hamilton addressed specific Anti-Federalist criticisms about federal jurisdiction over suits between citizens of different states and over equity cases, in which judges based their decisions not on a body of law but on broad principles of fairness. The range of the jurisdiction granted to the federal courts, Hamilton argued, was required to ensure the supremacy of federal law, the protection of equal rights for citizens in each state, and the government's ability to deal with foreign nations.

Hamilton and other Federalists assured skeptical critics that the most highly qualified individuals would serve as federal judges and that the new Congress would organize the nation's court system in ways that protected traditional liberties, such as the trial by jury. Yet even many who supported ratification of the Constitution remained concerned that the provisions for the judiciary failed to provide institutional protections of established legal rights and procedures.

6. Ratification

In several states, the conventions voting to ratify the Constitution passed resolutions suggesting amendments that should be added to the Constitution. Those related to the judiciary aimed to protect the right to a jury trial, to forbid appeals to the Supreme Court based on the facts rather than the law in a case, and to restrict the jurisdiction of the federal courts so as to protect citizens from distant court appearances in suits regarding small amounts of money. Virginia's convention wanted an amendment that limited the jurisdiction of any lower federal courts to admiralty matters and left for the state courts most federal questions. Several of the conventions incorporated their proposed amendments in a bill of rights that they wanted to attach to the Constitution.

7. Judiciary Act of 1789

When Congress turned early in its first session to the organization of the federal courts, the ratification debates had a significant impact on the proposals for the federal judicial system. The Judiciary Act of September 1789 represented a compromise that established a three-tier system of federal courts with broad jurisdiction that at the same time allowed the state courts to share jurisdiction over many matters arising under federal law and the Constitution. In addition to a Supreme Court, the federal judiciary included district courts that exercised jurisdiction over admiralty cases and minor criminal cases and civil suits, and circuit courts that served as the principal trial courts with jurisdiction over most federal crimes, disputes between citizens of different states, suits involving the government, and some appeals from the district courts. The procedures to be used in the federal courts, including rules for jury selection, would generally follow the practices of the state in which the federal court met. The provisions for the federal circuit courts, with the often-burdensome requirement that Supreme Court justices regularly preside in these regional courts, were a response to the pervasive fears that a federal judiciary would be too remote from most citizens and would eradicate regional legal customs.

8. The Bill of Rights

The defined structure of the federal judiciary was not enough to eliminate the doubts raised by the Anti-Federalists and shared by many other Americans. As the Senate considered the proposed judiciary bill, James Madison in the House of Representatives presented a draft of a bill of rights that would guarantee many of the legal protections demanded by critics of the Constitution. Madison's proposed amendments emphasized civil liberties and the rights of criminal defendants rather than the restructuring of the judiciary that had been advocated by some of the draft bills of rights. The amendments, ten of which were ratified in 1791, directly responded to debates on the proposed judiciary by affirming through the Sixth and Seventh Amendments the right to criminal and civil jury trials, with provision for criminal juries to be drawn from the district in which the crime was committed, and by prohibiting reexamination of facts determined by a jury.

Debates would continue, and go on even today, about the proper organization of the federal courts and the reach of federal jurisdiction, but the Judiciary Act of 1789 and the Bill of Rights combined to secure a measure of public confidence in the new Constitution and the unprecedented system of federal courts.

Part II. Constitutional Origins of the Federal Judiciary—Suggested Discussion Questions

1. One of the recurring debates in the Federal Convention concerned the power to appoint federal judges to their lifetime positions. How might the judiciary have developed differently if the Constitution had granted either the President or the Congress exclusive authority to appoint judges?
(See document II in accompanying Historical Documents.)

2. The Council of Revision proposed by James Madison would have given federal judges and the President a joint role in approving or vetoing acts of Congress before they went into effect. How would the Council of Revision have altered the checks and balances in the federal government? What effect would the Council of Revision have had on the independence of the federal judiciary?
(See document III in accompanying Historical Documents.)

3. In a constitutional government based on popular sovereignty, what role does the judiciary play in protecting the will of the people?

4. No court system in the states, the colonies, or Great Britain had been as independent of the other branches of government as was the judiciary outlined in Article III of the Constitution. How did the Constitution protect the independence of federal judges? Why did the framers of the Constitution think this independence was necessary?

5. Anti-Federalists feared that the establishment of a federal judiciary, with federal trial courts in all the states, would lead to the elimination of state courts. Federalists, on the other hand, argued that a system of federal trial courts with broad jurisdiction was necessary to guarantee the equal rights of all citizens, regardless of state residence. How did the federal court system established by the Constitution and the Judiciary Act of 1789 balance the need for a uniform, national court system with a regard for the state judiciaries?

6. During the ratification debates, the most widespread criticism of the judicial system outlined by the proposed Constitution was that it would not protect the traditional rights to a jury trial. Why was the jury trial considered so important? How could the Constitution be amended to protect the juries' role in the federal courts?

Part III. Constitutional Origins of the Federal Judiciary—Historical Documents

In the Federal Convention, 1787

1. The Virginia Plan on the Judiciary

8. Resolved, that the Executive and a convenient number of the National Judiciary, ought to compose a council of revision with authority to examine every act of the National Legislature before it shall operate, & every act of a particular Legislature before a Negative thereon shall be final; and that the dissent of the said Council shall amount to a rejection, unless the Act of the National Legislature be again passed, or that of a particular Legislature be again negatived by ____ of the members of each branch.

9. Resolved, that a National Judiciary be established to consist of one or more supreme tribunals, and of inferior tribunals to be chosen by the National Legislature, to hold their offices during good behavior; and to receive punctually at stated times fixed compensation for their services, in which no increase or diminution shall be made so as to affect the persons actually in office at the time of such increase or diminution. that the jurisdiction of the inferior tribunals shall be to hear & determine in the first instance, and of the supreme tribunal to hear and determine in the dernier resort, all piracies & felonies on the high seas, captures from an enemy; cases in which foreigners or citizens of other States applying to such jurisdictions may be interested, or which respect the collection of the National revenue; impeachments of any National officers, and questions which may involve the national peace and harmony.

[Document Source: *Records of the Federal Convention*, ed., Farrand, 1: 21-22. (spelling modernized)]

2. Appointment Power

Resol. 11. "that a National Judiciary be established to consist of one supreme tribunal." agreed to nem. con. [unanimously]
 "The Judges of which to be appointed by the 2d. branch [the Senate] of the National Legislature."
 Mr. Gorham, would prefer an appointment by the 2d branch [the Senate] to an appointment by the whole Legislature; but he thought even that branch too numerous, and too little personally responsible, to ensure a good choice. He suggested that the Judges be appointed by the Executive with the advice & consent of the 2d branch, in the mode prescribed by the constitution of Massachusetts. This

mode had been long practised in that country, & was found to answer perfectly well.

Mr. Wilson, still would prefer an appointment by the Executive; but if that could not be attained, would prefer in the next place, the mode suggested by Mr. Gorham. He thought it his duty however to move in the first instance "that the Judges be appointed by the Executive." Mr. Gouvernour Morris 2ded. the motion.

Mr. Luther Martin was strenuous for an appointment by the 2d. branch. Being taken from all the States it would be best informed of characters & most capable of making a fit choice.

Mr. Sherman concurred in the observations of Mr. Martin, adding that the Judges ought to be diffused, which would be more likely to be attended to by the 2d. branch, than by the Executive.

Mr Mason. The mode of appointing the Judges may depend in some degree on the mode of trying impeachments, of the Executive. If the Judges were to form a tribunal for that purpose, they surely ought not to be appointed by the Executive. There were insuperable objections besides against referring the appointment to the Executive. He mentioned as one, that as the seat of Government must be in some one State, and the Executive would remain in office for a considerable time, for 4, 5, or 6 years at least he would insensibly form local & personal attachments within the particular State that would deprive equal merit elsewhere, of an equal chance of promotion.

Mr. Gorham. As the Executive will be responsible in point of character at least, for a judicious and faithful discharge of his trust, he will be careful to look through all the States for proper characters.—The Senators will be as likely to form their attachments at the seat of Government where they reside, as the Executive. If they can not get the man of the particular State to which they may respectively belong, they will be indifferent to the rest. Public bodies feel no personal responsibly and give full play to intrigue & cabal. . . .

Mr. Madison, suggested that the Judges might be appointed by the Executives with the concurrence of 1/3 at least of the 2d. branch. This would unite the advantage of responsibility in the Executive with the security afforded in the 2d. branch against any incautious or corrupt nomination by the Executive.

Mr. Sherman, was clearly for an election by the Senate. It would be composed of men nearly equal to the Executive, and would of course have on the whole more wisdom. They would bring into their deliberations a more diffusive knowledge of characters. It would be less easy for candidates to intrigue with them, than with the Executive Magistrate. For these reasons he thought there would be a better security for a proper choice in the Senate than in the Executive.

Mr. Randolph. It is true that when the appointment of the Judges was vested in the 2d. branch an equality of votes had not been given to it. Yet he had rather leave the appointment there than give it to the Executive. He thought the advantage of personal responsibility might be gained in the Senate by requiring the respective votes of the members to be entered on the Journal. He thought too that the hope of receiving appointments would be more diffusive if they depended on the Senate, the members of which would be diffusively known, than if they depended on a single man who could not be personally known to a very great extent; and consequently that opposition to the System, would be so far weakened

Mr. Bedford thought there were solid reasons against leaving the appointment to the Executive. He must trust more to information than the Senate. It would put it in his power to gain over the larger States, by gratifying them with a preference of their Citizens. The responsibility of the Executive so much talked of was chimerical. He could not be punished for mistakes.

Mr. Gorham remarked that the Senate could have no better information than the Executive. They must like him, trust to information from the members belonging to the particular State where the Candidate resided. The Executive would certainly be more answerable for a good appointment, as the whole blame of a bad one would fall on him alone. He did not mean that he would be answerable under any other penalty than that of public censure, which with honorable minds was a sufficient one.

[Document Source: *Records of the Federal Convention*, ed., Farrand, 2: 41–43. (spelling modernized)]

3. Council of Revision

Mr. Wilson moved as an amendment to Resoln: 10. that the supreme National Judiciary should be associated with the Executive in the Revisionary power. This proposition had been before made, and failed; but he was so confirmed by reflection in the opinion of its utility, that he thought it incumbent on him to make another effort: The Judiciary ought to have an opportunity of remonstrating against projected encroachments on the people as well as on themselves. It had been said that the Judges, as expositors of the Laws would have an opportunity of defending their constitutional rights. There was weight in this observation; but this power of the Judges did not go far enough. Laws may be unjust, may be unwise, may be dangerous, may be destructive; and yet not be so unconstitutional as to justify the Judges in refusing to give them effect. Let them have a share in the Revisionary power, and they will have an opportunity of taking notice of these characters of a law, and of counteracting, by the weight of their opinions the improper views of the Legislature.—Mr Madison 2ded. the motion

Mr Gorham did not see the advantage of employing the Judges in this way. As Judges they are not to be presumed to possess any peculiar knowledge of the mere policy of public measures. Nor can it be necessary as a security for their constitutional rights. The Judges in England have no such additional provision for their defence, yet their jurisdiction is not invaded. He thought it would be best to let the Executive alone be responsible, and at most to authorize him to call on Judges for their opinions,

Mr. Ellsworth approved heartily of the motion. The aid of the Judges will give more wisdom & firmness to the Executive. They will possess a systematic and accurate knowledge of the Laws, which the Executive can not be expected always to possess. The law of Nations also will frequently come into question. Of this the Judges alone will have competent information.

Mr. Madison considered the object of the motion as of great importance to the meditated Constitution. It would be useful to the Judiciary department giving it an additional opportunity of defending itself against legislative encroachments; It would be useful to the Executive, by inspiring additional confidence & firmness in exerting the revisionary power: It would be useful to the Legislature by the valuable assistance it would give in preserving a consistency, conciseness, perspicuity & technical propriety in the laws, qualities peculiarly necessary; & yet shamefully wanting in our republican Codes. It would moreover be useful to the Community at large as an additional check against a pursuit of those unwise & unjust measures which constituted so great a portion of our calamities. If any solid objection could be urged against the motion, it must be on the supposition that it tended to give too much strength either to the Executive or Judiciary. He did not think there was the least ground for this apprehension. It was much more to be apprehended that notwithstanding this co-operation of the two departments, the Legislature would still be an overmatch for them. Experience in all the States had evinced a powerful tendency in the Legislature to absorb all power into its vortex. This was the real source of danger to the American Constitutions; & suggested the necessity of giving every defensive authority to the other departments that was consistent with republican principles.

. . .

Mr. Gerry did not expect to see this point which had undergone full discussion, again revived. The object he conceived of the Revisionary power was merely to secure the Executive department against legislative encroachment. The Executive therefore who will best know and be ready to defend his rights ought alone to have the defence of them. The motion was liable to strong objections. It was combining & mixing together the Legislative & the other departments. It was establishing an improper coalition between the Executive & Judiciary departments. It was making Statesmen of the Judges; and setting them up as the guardians of the Rights of the people. He relied for his part on the Representatives of the people as the guardians of their Rights & interests. It was making the Expositors of the Laws, the Legislators which ought never to be done. A better expedient for correcting the laws, would be to appoint as had been done in Pennsylvania a person or persons of proper skill, to draw bills for the Legislature.

. . .

Col Mason Observed that the defence of the Executive was not the sole object of the Revisionary power. He expected even greater advantages from it. Notwithstanding the precautions taken in the Constitution of the Legislature, it would so much resemble that of the individual States, that it must be expected frequently to pass unjust and pernicious laws. This restraining power was therefore essentially necessary. It would have the effect not only of hindering the final passage of such laws; but would discourage demagogues from attempting to get them passed. It had been said (by Mr. L. Martin) that if the Judges were joined in this check on the laws, they would have a double negative, since in their expository capacity of Judges they would have one negative. He would reply that in this capacity they could impede in one case only, the operation of laws. They could declare an unconstitutional law void. But with regard to every law however unjust oppressive or pernicious, which did not come plainly under this description, they would be under the necessity as Judges to give it a free course. He wished the further use to be made of the Judges, of giving aid in preventing every improper law. Their aid will be the more valuable as they are in the habit and practice of considering laws in their true principles, and in all their consequences.

. . .

Mr. Gorham. All agree that a check on the Legislature is necessary. But there are two objections against admitting the Judges to share in it which no observations on the other side seem to obviate. the 1st. is that the Judges ought to carry into the exposition of the laws no prepossessions with regard to them. 2d. that as the Judges will outnumber the Executive, the revisionary check would be thrown entirely out of the Executive hands, and instead of enabling him to defend himself, would enable the Judges to sacrifice him.

. . .

Mr. Rutledge thought the Judges of all men the most unfit to be concerned in the revisionary Council. The Judges ought never to give their opinion on a law till it comes before them. He thought it equally unnecessary. The Executive could advise with the officers of State, as of war, finance &c. and avail himself of their information and opinions.

On Question on Mr. Wilson's motion for joining the Judiciary in the Revision of laws it passed in the negative—

[Document Source: *Records of the Federal Convention*, ed., Farrand, 2: 73–80. (spelling modernized)]

4. Article III of the U.S. Constitution

Section. 1. The judicial Power of the United States, shall be vested in one supreme Court, and in such inferior Courts as the Congress may from time to time ordain and establish. The Judges, both of the supreme and inferior Courts, shall hold their Offices during good Behaviour, and shall, at stated Times, receive for their Services, a Compensation, which shall not be diminished during their Continuance in Office.

Section. 2. The judicial Power shall extend to all Cases, in Law and Equity, arising under this Constitution, the Laws of the United States, and Treaties made, or which shall be made, under their Authority;—to all Cases affecting Ambassadors, other public Ministers and Consuls;—to all Cases of admiralty and maritime Jurisdiction;—to Controversies to which the United States shall be a Party;—to Controversies between two or more States;—between a State and Citizens of another State;—between Citizens of different States;—between Citizens of the same State claiming Lands under Grants of different States, and between a State, or the Citizens thereof, and foreign States, Citizens or Subjects.

In all Cases affecting Ambassadors, other public Ministers and Consuls, and those in which a State shall be Party, the supreme Court shall have original Jurisdiction. In all the other Cases before mentioned, the supreme Court shall have appellate Jurisdiction, both as to Law and Fact, with such Exceptions, and under such Regulations as the Congress shall make.

The Trial of all Crimes, except in Cases of Impeachment, shall be by Jury; and such Trial shall be held in the State where the said Crimes shall have been committed; but when not committed within any State, the Trial shall be at such Place or Places as the Congress may by Law have directed.

Section. 3. Treason against the United States, shall consist only in levying War against them, or in adhering to their Enemies, giving them Aid and Comfort. No Person shall be convicted of Treason unless on the Testimony of two Witnesses to the same overt Act, or on Confession in open Court.

The Anti-Federalist Critique

5. Letters of "Brutus"

The judicial power of the United States is to be vested in a supreme court, and in such inferior courts as Congress may from time to time ordain and establish. The powers of these courts are very extensive; and their jurisdiction comprehends all civil causes, except such as arise between citizens of the same state; and it extends to all cases in law and equity arising under the constitution. . . . It is easy to see, that in the common course of things, these courts will eclipse the dignity, and take away from the respectability, of the state courts. These courts will be, in themselves, totally independent of the states, deriving their authority from the United States, and receiving from them fixed salaries; and in the course of human events it is to be expected, that they will swallow up all the powers of the courts in the respective states.
New York Journal, October 18, 1787.

The real effect of this system of government, will therefore be brought home to the feelings of the people, through the medium of the judicial power. It is, moreover, of great importance, to examine with care the nature and extent of the judicial power, because those who are to be vested with it, are to be placed in a situation altogether unprecedented in a free county. They are to be rendered totally independent, both of the people and the legislature, both with respect to their offices and salaries. No errors they may commit can be corrected by any power above them, if any such power there be, nor can they be removed from office for making ever so many erroneous adjudications.
New York Journal, January 31, 1788.

[Document Sources: *The Debate on the Constitution*, ed., Bailyn, 1: 168, 2: 129.]

6. Letters from the Federal Farmer

. . . The supreme court shall have jurisdiction both as to law and fact. What is meant by court? Is the jury included in the term, or is it not? I conceive it is not included: and so the members of the convention, I am very sure, understand it. . . .

As the trial by jury is provided for in criminal causes, I shall confine my observations to civil causes – and in these, I hold it is the established right of the jury by the common law, and the fundamental laws of this country, to give a general verdict in all cases when they choose to do it, to decide both as to law and fact whenever blended together in the issue put to them. . . .

The jury trial, especially politically considered, is by far the most important feature in the judicial department in a free country, and the right in question is far the most valuable part, and the last that ought to be yielded, of this trial. Juries are constantly and frequently drawn from the body of the people, and freemen of the country; and by holding the jury's right to return a general verdict in all cases sacred, we secure to the people at large, their just and rightful control of the judicial department. If the conduct of judges shall be severe and arbitrary, and tend to subvert the laws, and change the forms of government, the jury may check them, by deciding against their opinions and determinations, in similar cases.

[Document Source: *The Complete Anti-Federalist*, ed., Storing, 2: 319–20.]

The Federalist Defense

7. Federalist 78 (Excerpt)

For I agree that "there is no liberty, if the power of judging be not separated from the legislative and executive powers." And it proves, in the last place, that as liberty can have nothing to fear from the judiciary alone, but would have every thing to fear from its union with either of the other departments, . . . and that as nothing can contribute so much to its firmness and independence, as permanency in office, this quality may therefore be justly regarded as an indispensable ingredient in its constitution; and in a great measure as the citadel of the public justice and the public security.

The complete independence of the courts of justice is peculiarly essential in a limited constitution. By limited constitution I understand one which contains certain specified exceptions to the legislative authority; such for instance as that it shall pass no bills of attainder, no *ex post facto* laws, and the like. Limitations of this kind can be preserved in practice no other way than through the medium of the courts of justice; whose duty it must be to declare all acts contrary to the manifest tenor of the constitution void. Without this, all the reservations of particular rights or privileges would amount to nothing.

[Document Source: *The Debate on the Constitution*, ed., Bailyn, 2: 469.]

8. Federalist 80 (Excerpt)

It may be esteemed the basis of the union, that "the citizens of each state shall be entitled to all the privileges and immunities of citizens of the several states." And if it be a just principle that every government *ought to possess the means of executing its own provisions by its own authority*, it will follow, that in order to the inviolable maintenance of that equality of privileges and immunities to which the citizens of the union will be entitled, the national judiciary ought to preside in all cases in which one state or its citizens are opposed to another state or its citizens. To secure the full effect of so fundamental a provision against all evasion and subterfuge, it is necessary that its construction should be committed to that tribunal, which, having no local attachments, will be likely to be impartial between the different states and their citizens, and which, owing its official existence to the union, will never be likely to feel any bias inauspicious to the principles on which it is founded.

[Document Source: *The Debate on the Constitution*, ed., Bailyn, 2: 479.]

9. Federalist 81 (Excerpt)

The amount of the observation hitherto made on the authority of the judicial department is this—that it has been carefully restricted to those causes which are manifestly proper for the cognizance of the national judicature, that in the partition of this authority a very small portion of original jurisdiction has been reserved to the supreme court, and the rest consigned to the subordinate tribunals—that the supreme court will possess an appellate jurisdiction both as to law and fact in all cases referred to them, but subject to any *exceptions* and *regulations* which may be thought adviseable; that this appellate jurisdiction does in no case *abolish* the trial by jury, and that an ordinary degree of prudence and integrity in the national councils will insure us solid advantages from the establishment of the proposed judiciary, without exposing us to any of the inconveniences which have been predicted from that source.

[Document Source: *The Debate on the Constitution*, ed., Bailyn, 2: 492.]

Bibliography

The Complete Anti-Federalist. Herbert J. Storing, ed. 7 vols. Chicago: University of Chicago Press, 1981.

The Debate on the Constitution: Federalist and Anti-Federalist Speeches, Articles, and Letters During the Struggle over Ratification. Bernard Bailyn, ed. 2 vols. New York: Library of America, 1993.

The Records of the Federal Convention of 1787. Max Farrand, ed. 3 vols. 1911. Reprint, New Haven: Yale University Press, 1966.

www.ingramcontent.com/pod-product-compliance
Lightning Source LLC
Chambersburg PA
CBHW080535190526
45169CB00008B/3180